America's First Wilderness

New York's Forest Preserves

Norman J. Van Valkenburgh

PURPLE MOUNTAIN PRESS
Fleischmanns, New York

First Edition 2008

Published by Purple Mountain Press, Ltd.
P.O. Box 309, Fleischmanns, New York 12430-0309
845-254-4062, 845-254-4476 (fax), purple@catskill.net
http://www.catskill.net/purple

Copyright © 2008 by Norman J. Van Valkenburgh

All rights reserved under International and Pan-American Copyright Conventions. No part of this book may be reproduced or transmitted by any means without permission in writing from the publisher.

ISBN-13: 978-1-930098-88-6
ISBN: 1-930098-88-X

Cover: Looking west-northwesterly across the Ashokan Reservoir into Maltby Hollow and at the distant Catskill peaks of (left to right) Balsam Cap, Friday, Cornell, and Wittenberg with Hanover Mountain in the left foreground and the shoulder of Samuel's Point on the right. Courtesy Aaron Bennett.

Title page: Eastern escarpment of the Catskills from Huckleberry Point. Courtesy of the Catskill Center for Conservation and Development.

Illustration credits

Adirondack Mountain Club (ADK), www.adk.org., pages 3, 41. Adirondack Research Library of the Association for the Protection of the Adirondacks, pages 6, 7, 8, 10, 11, 13, 14, 15, 21, 24, 25, 27, 28, 30, 31, 33 (left), 34 (top—photo by Ken Rimany), 39, 40, 42 (campers, snowshoer). The Catskill Center for Conservation and Development, pages 9, 16, 18, 19, 29, 33 (right), 34 (bottom), 35, 42 (fishing, canoeing), 43. Lowville Free Library, page 12. Minneapolis Institute of Arts, Bequest of Mrs. Lillian Lawhead Rinderer in memory of her brother, William A. Lawhead, and the William Hood Dunwoody Fund, painting by Jasper Francis Cropsey, page 23. Crystal Bridges Museum of American Art, Bentonville, Arkansas, painting by Asher B. Durand, 1849, oil on canvas, 44 x 36 inches, page 37. All other illustrations are from the author's collection.

Manufactured in the United States of America on acid-free paper.

The Adirondack Forest Preserve and Adirondack Park are often confused. So too are the Catskill Forest Preserve and Catskill Park. Why are each different?

The Adirondack Forest Preserve is the <u>state-owned land</u> in the twelve counties of Clinton, Essex, Franklin, Fulton, Hamilton, Herkimer, Lewis, Oneida, St. Lawrence, Saratoga, Warren, and Washington. The Adirondack Park is <u>all the land</u> within a boundary shown on maps as a blue line including all of Essex and Hamilton counties and parts of the other ten counties.

The Catskill Forest Preserve is the <u>state-owned land</u> in the four counties of Delaware, Greene, Sullivan, and Ulster. The Catskill Park is <u>all the land</u> within a boundary shown on maps as a blue line including parts of these four counties.

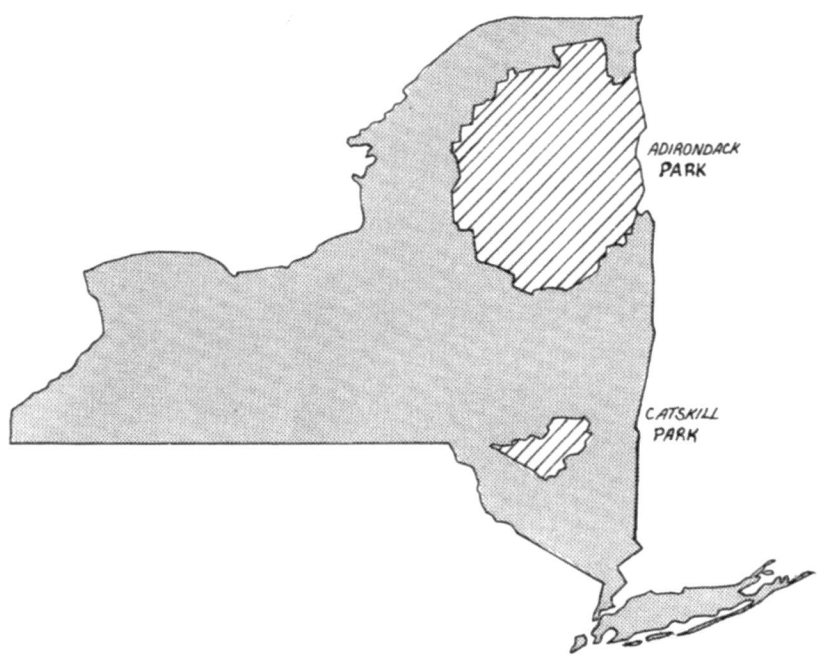

3

Chap. 283.

AN ACT to establish a forest commission, and to define its powers and duties and for the preservation of forests.

Passed May 15, 1885; three-fifths being present.

The People of the State of New York, represented in Senate and Assembly, do enact as follows:

Forest commission to be appointed by governor, etc.

SECTION 1. There shall be a forest commission which shall consist of three persons who shall be styled forest commissioners, and who may be removed by the governor for cause. The forest commissioners shall be appointed by the governor by and with the advice and consent of the senate.

Terms of office.

§ 2. At the first meeting of the forest commissioners they shall divide themselves by lot, so that the term of one shall expire in two years, one in four years, and one in six years from the first day of February next ensuing. Except as to the three terms of office thus determined, the term of office of a forest commissioner shall be six years from the first day of February on which the preceding term expires.

Future appointments.

§ 3. During the month of January, in the year eighteen hundred and eighty-eight, and in every second year thereafter, the governor by and with the advice and consent of the senate shall appoint one forest commissioner.

Vacancies.

Vacancies that may exist in the office of a forest commissioner after the commencement of a term of office shall be filled by the governor's appointment subject to the confirmation of the senate at its next session for the unexpired portion of the term in which the vacancy occurs.

To serve without compensation.

§ 4. The forest commissioners shall serve without compensation except that there shall be paid them their reasonable expenses incurred in the performance of their official duties.

Forest warden, inspectors, etc.

§ 5. The forest commission shall have power to employ a forest warden, forest inspectors, a clerk and all such agents, as they may deem necessary, and to fix their compensations, but the expenses and salaries of such warden, agents, clerk, inspectors and assistants shall not exceed in the aggregate with the other expenses of the commission the sum therefor appropriated by the legislature.

Office for.

§ 6. The trustees of public buildings, under chapter three hundred and forty-nine, laws of eighteen hundred and eighty-three, shall provide rooms for office for the forest commission, with proper furniture and fixtures, and with warming and lights.

Lands to be known as forest preserve.

§ 7. All the lands now owned or which may hereafter be acquired by the state of New York, within the counties of Clinton, excepting the towns of Altona and Dannemora, Essex, Franklin, Fulton, Hamilton, Herkimer, Lewis, Saratoga, St. Lawrence, Warren, Washington, Greene, Ulster and Sullivan, shall constitute and be known as the forest preserve.

To be kept as wild forest lands.

§ 8. The lands now or hereafter constituting the forest preserve shall be forever kept as wild forest lands. They shall not be sold, nor shall they be leased or taken by any person or corporation, public or private.

Powers and duties of commission.

§ 9. The forest commission shall have the care, custody, control and superintendence of the forest preserve. It shall be the duty of the commission to maintain and protect the forests now on the forest preserve, and to promote as far as practicable the further growth of forests

Much of the history of New York's Forest Preserves and Parks is told in the words of various laws and in the state's constitution.

Laws begin as bills written by the New York State Assembly and Senate. A bill introduced in these two houses or chambers of the legislature is debated until both agree on its wording. Once it passes both houses, a bill is sent to the governor. The governor may sign the bill at which point it becomes law. He may reject the bill (officially called a veto) and there it dies. He may elect to neither sign nor reject the bill but let it sit on his desk. After a specified time, the bill then becomes law without the governor's signature.

An amendment to the constitution follows the same track through the legislature. If approved by two successive legislatures, it is put on the ballot at the next November election when the voters of the state either approve or reject the amendment.

Sometimes the constitution is reviewed, rewritten, amended, etc. by a constitutional convention made up of delegates appointed from all across the state. Once a new or reworded constitution is approved by a convention, it is put before the voters at the next election when it may be either approved or rejected.

Copy of 1885 law that created the Forest Preserve (see Sections 7&8).

Today's New Yorkers may not realize the debt they owe to a few men of vision of an earlier time. Without their efforts water taps might run dry; the mountains of the Adirondacks and the Catskills might not be covered with forests; the woods and fields of the hillsides might be empty of wildlife and woodland plants and flowers. Who were these men and why did they speak out?

Above:
Early print of Mount Haystack, Adirondack Mountains.

Facing page:
Early (1873) map of land patents of the Adirondacks.

In July of 1776, Britain's thirteen North American colonies declared their independence. The State of New York then became the owner of seven-million acres of lands and waters extending from the Canadian border on the north to the Mohawk River on the south and from Lake Ontario on the west to Lake Champlain and Vermont on the east and including all of the Adirondack Mountains. The law that made it official said these lands "for ever after shall be vested in the people of this State. . . ." But "for ever" didn't last long.

In the years that followed, New York State enacted a series of laws to dispose of what were called "waste" lands. By 1820, nearly all of the Adirondack lands had been sold to private owners.

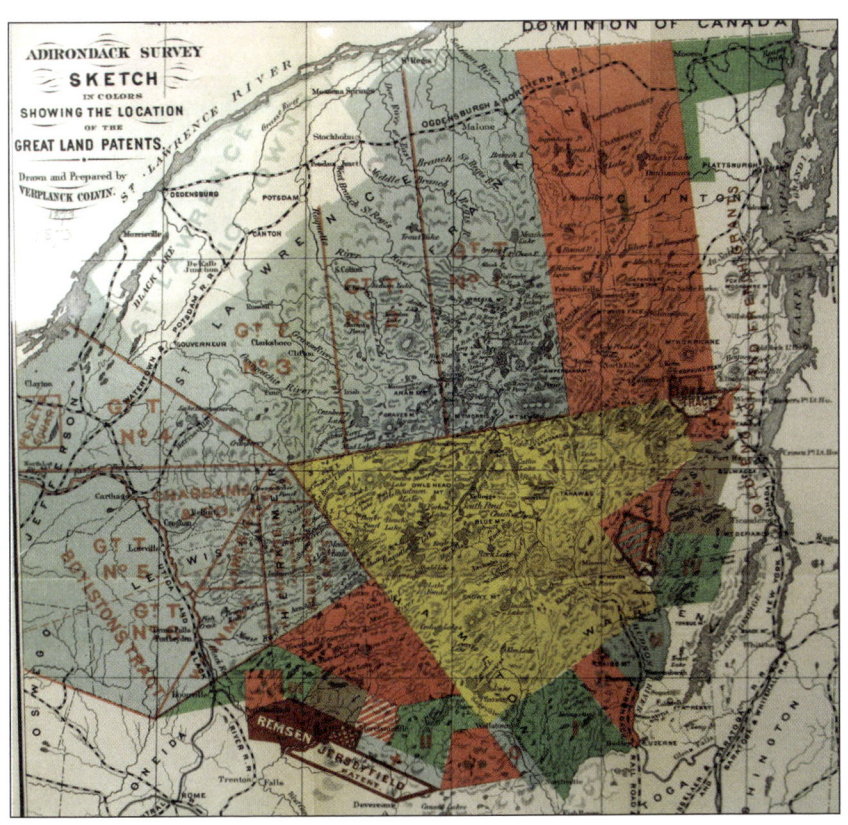

The new owners of the former public lands were not interested in the future. They wanted the quick profit they could make from the natural resources on those lands. Loggers stripped away the trees and left behind eroded hillsides and muddy streams. Timber thieves cut the forests on what state land was left. Forest fires followed and destroyed the remaining natural cover. Settlements and farms further cleared the land. In the Catskills, tanners cut the hemlocks taking only the bark and leaving behind the skeletons of these once-majestic trees.

In spite of all this, deer and other animals roamed the mountains. Fish swam the streams, lakes, and ponds. The so-called "sportsmen" of the day soon arrived. Stories of catching 120 pounds of trout in two hours, of shooting five deer in a month, of catching a nineteen-pound trout came to be told. The stories were true. Like the forests, the numbers of animals and fish declined. Some, like the lynx, the wolf, and the panther disappeared, never to return. By 1850, the vast wilderness was nearly gone. People of vision were needed and their voices began to be heard.

S. H. (Samuel H.) Hammond, an Albany attorney and sportsman, wrote in his 1857 *Wild Northern Scenes* that the Adirondacks was a place "which civilization with its improvements and its rush of progress has not yet invaded. . . . Had I my way, I would mark out a circle of a hundred miles in diameter, and throw around it the protecting aegis of the constitution. I would make it a forest forever."

An 1864 *New York Times* editorial suggested that concerned citizens band together and "seizing upon the choicest of the Adirondack Mountains, before they are despoiled of their forests, make of them grand parks, owned in common. . . ."

Original cover of Wild Northern Scenes.

George Perkins Marsh was born (in 1801) and raised in Vermont. Educated in the law at Dartmouth College in New Hampshire, he later became interested in literature and languages (he could speak twenty) and in the natural sciences.

In 1861, after serving in a number of academic and governmental posts, President Abraham Lincoln appointed him minister to Italy, a position he held until his death in 1882. In 1864, Marsh published *Man and Nature* which detailed the role man played in shaping Earth's environment. He argued that the destruction of forests led to a diminished water supply and would change a once-lush landscape to desert. Marsh and his works were not directly related to the Adirondacks but influenced others who used his theories to speak on behalf of these northern mountains.

**Portrait of George Perkins Marsh (1861)
from the camera of Mathew Brady.**

Franklin B. Hough (pronounced Huff), a country doctor, settled in Lowville, Lewis County, on the western edge of the Adirondacks. At the age of twenty-four, he published a *Catalog of Plants of Lewis County*. Called "the pioneer author of county histories of New York," he wrote histories of St. Lawrence, Franklin, Jefferson, and Lewis Counties and compiled a *Gazetteer of New York*. He is best remembered as the "father of American forestry."

While superintendent of the New York State census of 1855 and again in 1865, he traveled throughout the Adirondacks and saw firsthand the destruction of the forests. In 1873, he delivered his paper "The Duty of Governments in the Preservation of Forests" before the American Association for the Advancement of Science. He was later appointed the first forestry agent in the U.S. Department of Agriculture. This single position grew into the U.S. Forest Service.

The historical marker in front of the Hough home reads: "1885-1935—HOUGH HOME—The Forest Act of 1885 was enacted largely because of the vision and efforts of Franklin B. Hough, first New York forester."

Verplanck Colvin studied for the law in his father's office in Albany. While working with the deeds written there, he became interested in the boundaries of the parcels and tracts of land described in them. He was fascinated with the large grants of land in the Adirondacks and prepared a map showing their location. In 1865, he went to the mountains to check his work. He wrote he "was amazed at the natural park like beauty of this wilderness."

In 1870, he climbed to the summit of Mt. Seward, a mountain in the High Peaks region of the Adirondacks. In a report to the Board of Regents of the State of New York, he described the view from the top of the mountain "as magnificent, yet differing from other of the loftier Adirondacks, in that no clearings were discernible; wilderness everywhere; lake on lake, river on river, mountain on mountain, numberless."

He stressed the need to preserve the forests to assure a future water supply and recommended that an "ADIRONDACK PARK or timber reserve" be created.

Sketch by Verplanck Colvin of some of the
men of his survey crew at work.

Responding to these concerns, an 1872 law created a Commission of State Parks to consider the benefits of the state purchasing "the timbered regions" in a number of Adirondack counties "and converting the same into a public park."

Among those named to the commission were Franklin Hough and Verplanck Colvin. The commission's report concluded: "we are of opinion that the protection of a great portion of that [Adirondack] forest from wanton destruction is absolutely and immediately required." The report was filed and forgotten.

Colvin was not, however. He was given funding by another 1872 law "to aid in completing a survey of the Adirondack wilderness of New York. . . ."

In Colvin's 1872 report of his Adirondack survey, he described his discovery of "the summit water of the State, and the loftiest known and true high source of the Hudson River. . . ." He later named this "summit water" Lake Tear-of-the-Clouds and concluded "that within one hundred years, the cold, healthful living waters of the wilderness . . . will be required for the domestic water supply of the cities of the Hudson river valley." He was not far off the mark.

A thin blue line was drawn on a map of the Adirondacks inserted at the back of the report. Colvin wrote "this blue line . . . may be of value in the determination of the area of forest which it is necessary to preserve in order to protect . . . the source of the Hudson." This was the first blue line—twenty years before a later draftsman drew one around an Adirondack Park.

Verplanck Colvin's drawing of Lake Tear of the Clouds.

The view from Huckleberry Point looking westerly at the Catskill forests of the Indian Head Range and the Platte Clove Valley.

Finally, after New York State had sold or granted away most of its Adirondack "waste" lands, an 1883 law prohibited further sales of State lands in ten of the twelve Adirondack counties.

An 1884 law provided funding "for the employment of experts to investigate and report a system of forest preservation." The four members appointed to carry out the study came to be known as the Forestry Commission and, later, the Sargent Commission in recognition of its chairman, Charles S. Sargent.

Charles Sprague Sargent was graduated from Harvard College and was later Professor of Horticulture of Harvard University. He was instrumental in establishing the Arnold Arboretum and served as its director from 1873 till his death in 1927. He is especially noted as the author of *Silva of North America*, a fourteen-volume descriptive listing of every tree species in North America. When he was appointed to the Forestry Commission, Sargent was probably the foremost tree and forest expert in the country.

Charles Sprague Sargent

No previous mention had been made of the Catskills. In their investigation of a system of forest preservation, would Sargent and his fellow commissioners consider only the northern forest or would they look south to the mountains westerly from the Hudson River?

The Forestry Commission submitted its report in January of 1885 stating that "protection of rivers is the aim and excuse for forest ownership by the State; and the production of lumber should be made secondary. . . ." It went on to say, "It is of vital moment to the State to put an end to the temptation to strip the land of its forest wealth."

What of the Catskills? The commissioners did visit this "forest region" but disposed of it in a single paragraph. "The protection of these forests is, however, of less general importance than the preservation of the Adirondack forests. The possibility of their yielding merchantable timber again in any considerable quantities is at best remote; and they guard no streams of more than local influence." Really?

The commission proposed in the draft of a bill that:

> All the lands now owned or which may hereafter be acquired by the State of New York within the [eleven Adirondack] counties shall constitute and be known as the forest preserve. . . . The lands now or hereafter constituting the forest preserve shall be forever kept as wild forest lands.

These words live on yet today in New York State's Constitution and echo Samuel Hammond's early writing that these lands should be made "a forest forever."

**It was forests, streams, and sites such as this
that all three bills sought to protect.**

The report of the Forestry Commission, with its proposed bill, was directed to the New York State Legislature which asked Franklin Hough to prepare another bill. This proposed to manage the state lands as a forest crop to be harvested. Verplanck Colvin, working with Hough, favored preserving the forest in the form of a park. A third bill was written by Bernhard Fernow, a forester trained at the Prussian Forestry Academy, who later became chief of the federal Division of Forestry.

Yet another player stood in the background. Who was Cornelius Hardenbergh and where did he fit in this story of mountains, trees, streams, and forests?

Cornelius A. J. Hardenbergh was a farmer in southern Ulster County, one of the four Catskill counties. He was against taxes of any kind. When a tax was put on his wheel-making shop, he closed it rather than pay the tax.

Cornelius A. J. Hardenbergh

Hardenbergh was supervisor of his town and served on the Ulster County Board of Supervisors. Here he waged his longest battle against taxes. It began with a law requiring the county to pay taxes on its lands to the state. Another law directed the New York State Comptroller (or financial officer) to convey some other state lands to the county. The county was then to pay taxes on these lands. Hardenbergh saw to it that the county didn't pay the comptroller's tax bills.

In 1884, Hardenbergh was elected to the New York State Assembly. Together with Gilbert D. B. Hasbrouck, a fellow assemblyman from Ulster County, Hardenbergh prepared a bill that would settle the issue once and for all. It relieved Ulster County from the requirements of any previous law affecting taxes on its lands and conveyed the county lands to the state.

At about this time, the New York State Legislature was completing work on a proposed law to protect the state-owned Adirondack lands.

Governor David B. Hill

The bill approved by the legislature was signed into law by Governor David B. Hill on May 15, 1885. (See page 4.) It provided for a three-member Forest Commission and gave it authority to employ forest inspectors to watch over the state-owned lands and called for the appointment of forest wardens to protect the forest from fire. Today's wardens are known as forest rangers. It repeated the language from the Forestry Commission report and declared lands "now owned or which may hereafter be acquired by the state of New York . . . shall constitute and be known as the forest preserve" and assigned "care, custody, control and superintendence of the forest preserve" to a forest commission. It also declared that:

> The lands now or hereafter constituting the forest preserve shall be forever kept as wild forest lands. They shall not be sold, nor shall they be leased or taken by any person or corporation, public or private.

The language of the law then differed from that in the Forestry Commission report. The eleven Adirondack counties where the forest preserve would exist were listed. However, added at the end were the three Catskill counties of Greene, Ulster and Sullivan. Cornelius Hardenbergh had prevailed.

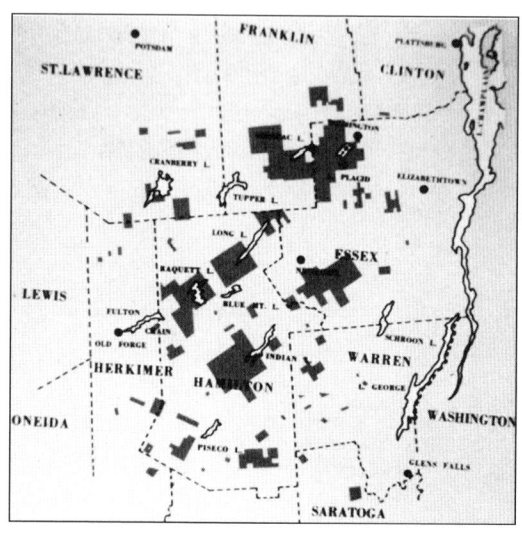

The original acreage (shaded) of the Adirondack Forest Preserve and the partial outline of the twelve Adirondack counties.

The original Adirondack Forest Preserve consisted of 681,374 acres. The Catskill Forest Preserve included 33,894 acres, all but about 1,000 acres being in Ulster County mostly on the slopes of Slide Mountain, the highest peak in the Catskills.

A second bill became law the next year. This stated that all "wild lands or forest lands belonging to or which may hereafter be acquired by the State . . . shall be assessed and taxed" at the same rate as private lands in the counties where they were located. Under this law, Ulster County still receives taxes from the State on those lands that were the subject of the long-running debate between Cornelius Hardenbergh and the state comptroller.

In 1887, Oneida County, on the southwestern fringe of the Adirondacks, was added to the list of Adirondack Forest Preserve counties. An 1888 law added Delaware County to the list of Catskill Forest Preserve counties. The number of Adirondack Forest Preserve counties still stands at twelve and the number of Catskill Forest Preserve counties remains at four.

Facing page: The historic Catskill Mountain House perched on the eastern escarpment of the Catskills overlooking the Hudson River Valley. The two lakes in the background are now the site of the state's North Lake-South Lake Public Campground.

A natural and changing forest maintains the high mountain sources of water that feed the streams, wetlands, lakes, ponds, and rivers of the state. These provide habitat for fish and other aquatic life as the forests do for the plants and animals of the uplands. Forests also improve the quality of the air breathed by the state's citizens and help to prevent climate change. Not many then understood these benefits.

Too few appreciated the sheer beauty of the forested, craggy mountains being pictured by Thomas Cole, Asher Durand, Jasper Cropsey, and others of the Hudson River School of Painting in their sweeping landscapes. Chances are none of the forest commissioners had studied George Perkins Marsh's *Man and Nature* and the lessons it taught.

So it was that the Forest Commission requested authority to sell the lands and timber of the Forest Preserve and to lease such lands for private campgrounds. The legislature responded and authorized the commission to sell "separate small parcels or tracts . . . of the Forest Preserve" and the timber on these state lands. Worse was yet to come.

In the annual reports of his Adirondack Survey, Verplanck Colvin wrote that a true park should be established within the Forest Preserve. Governor David Hill wanted a park in the "wilder portion of this region covering the mountains and lakes" of the Adirondacks but said parcels of the Forest Preserve should be leased to private owners. That didn't sound much like preservation.

The Forest Commission proposed that the state acquire and hold land in "one grand unbroken domain" and included a map in its 1891 report with a blue line indicating the boundary of an Adirondack Park. The idea of a blue line to outline the park was, of course, borrowed from Verplanck Colvin, who had drawn one on a map in his 1872 report to circle an area that "is necessary to preserve in order to protect . . . the source of the Hudson."

However, these proposals seemed to confuse forest preserve and park.

1891 Forest Commission map outlining a proposed Adirondack Park.

Concerns continued to be raised about the Forest Commission's administration of the Forest Preserve.

In response, the New York State Assembly undertook an investigation. It appointed a Committee on Public Lands and Forestry Concerning the Administration of Laws in Relation to the Forest Preserve by the Forest Commission.

The committee uncovered some questionable acts by at least one of the commissioners. It seems the commission had rejected all applications for exchanges of state land except those submitted by Everton Lumber Company. It then discovered that Commissioner Theodore Basselin was an agent of Everton. The committee also found an associate of Basselin's had consistently acquired valuable forest lands that were being sold to collect unpaid taxes while the state had not. Finally, the committee learned that Basselin was connected with other lumbering interests that had been favored by the Forest Commission.

The committee recommended more stringent laws and replacing the three-member Forest Commission with a commission of five members. Some observers thought this simply put five officials instead of three in a position to gain from the preserve's forest lands and timber.

This cover of the Forest Commission's report for the year 1890 lists Theodore B. Basselin as one of three commissioners. By this time, Basselin was in his sixth year as a manager with responsibility for the Forest Preserve.

During these early years, two significant funding bills were approved by the governor.

An 1890 law set aside the sum of $25,000 for the state to purchase lands within the forest preserve counties. These were the first monies provided for the acquisition of lands to add to the Forest Preserve. Over time, millions of dollars would be spent for this program.

An 1892 law allocated $250 "for completing the public path leading to the summit of Slide Mountain, Ulster County. . . ." This was the first authorization of a recreational trail and was the beginning of the extensive state trail system now running throughout the Adirondacks and Catskills.

Another 1892 law created the Adirondack Park. The new park was defined as the Forest Preserve lands within certain towns in the counties of Hamilton, Herkimer, St. Lawrence, Franklin, Essex, and Warren. The boundaries of the park followed the blue line on the map that had been in the 1891 Forest Commission report.

The designation had little, if any, effect on the state lands within the park. The private lands within the "blue line" were not affected in any way.

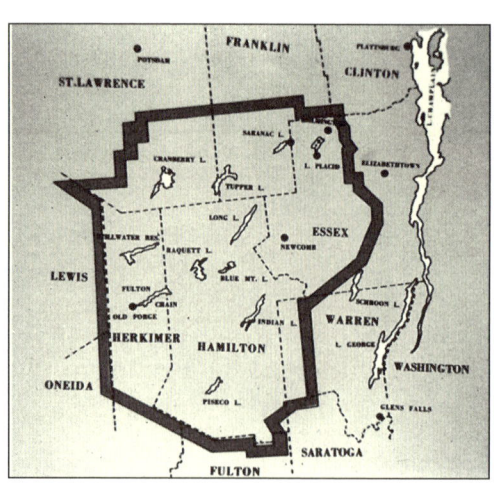

This map outlines the "blue line" of the original (1892) Adirondack Park.

This "cottage" on Phelps Island in Lake George seems to go beyond what was intended in the 1892 law.

Parts of the Adirondack Park law were decidedly negative. Section 4 authorized the Forest Commission to sell state-owned lands throughout the Adirondacks. Section 9 provided authority to lease "tracts of land within the limits of the Adirondack park . . . for the erection of camps or cottages. . . ."

The Forest Commission wasn't alone in proposing these programs. Governor Roswell P. Flower, in his message approving the law, wrote "all revenues from the sale of" the state lands "will be devoted to the purchase of new lands . . . the State preserve ought to pay the expense of its maintenance from the judicious sale of timber and the leasing, at moderate rentals, of small parcels of land to individuals for the establishment of summer homes. . . ."

Individuals and organizations in favor of preserving the forests and lands of the Adirondacks and Catskills were not happy. They hoped to change the way things were being done by working within the constitutional convention that was to begin in May of 1894.

Early in the proceedings of the 1894 Constitutional Convention, a Special Committee of State Forest Preservation was appointed. This five-member committee, chaired by David McClure, an attorney from New York City, issued a report stating:

> [I]t is necessary for the health, safety and general advantage of the people of the State that the forest lands now owned by and hereafter acquired by the State, and the timber on such lands, should be preserved intact as forest preserves, and not, under any circumstances, be sold.

It proposed that words to this effect be inserted in the constitution. This would protect the timber on the State lands, which had not been a part of earlier laws.

Long debates were held over various words offered to be included in the final proposal. McClure led much of the discussion stating, among other things: "we should not permit the sale of one acre of land. . . . We should not sell a tree or a branch of one. . . . The Legislature should purchase all of the forest lands, both in the Adirondacks and the Catskills. . . ."

O., I. No. 393, P. No. 452.—" The lands of the State now owned or hereafter acquired, constituting the forest preserves, shall be forever kept as wild forest land. They shall not, nor shall the timber thereon, be sold.

(Signed)   DAVID McCLURE,
Chairman.

REVISED RECORD
OF THE
CONSTITUTIONAL CONVENTION
OF THE
STATE OF NEW YORK

May 8, 1894, to September 29, 1894

REVISED BY
Hon. WILLIAM H. STEELE,
VICE-PRESIDENT OF THE CONSTITUTIONAL CONVENTION OF 1894.
Pursuant to Chap. 21, Laws of 1898.

PUBLISHED UNDER DIRECTION OF
Hon. CHARLES E. FITCH, L. H. D.,
SECRETARY OF THE CONSTITUTIONAL CONVENTION OF 1894.
Pursuant to Chap. 419, Laws of 1900.

342.747
Vol. II.

ALBANY:
THE ARGUS COMPANY, PRINTERS.
1900.

Many of the mountains and forests in this view of the magnificent distance of the Catskills, as seen from the Red Hill fire tower, are among those public lands protected by the Constitution of New York State.

The entire convention finally agreed on the language to be inserted in the new constitution:

> The lands of the State now owned or hereafter acquired, constituting the forest preserve as now fixed by law, shall be forever kept as wild forest lands. They shall not be leased, sold or exchanged, or be taken by any corporation, public or private, nor shall the timber thereon be sold, removed or destroyed.

This passed unanimously. At the General Election in November, the constitution was approved by a vote of 410,697 to 324,402 and took effect on January 1, 1895. The Forest Preserve section, with this same wording, survives in today's New York State Constitution.

Those concerned about the future of New York's mountain lands, forests, and waters were pleased with the protections written in the new constitution and that they would be "forever." But they also knew forever would last only as long as it took to amend the constitution.

The 1895 Legislature approved an amendment that would allow the sale or exchange of Forest Preserve land and the lease of such land for camps and cottages. The 1896 Legislature also approved the amendment, and it was put before the people of the state at the following general election. The voters soundly defeated the amendment, 710,505 against 321,486 in favor.

Proposals are still offered to change the protections of the Forest Preserve. Some reach the people for a decision. Amendments affecting all or a large part of the preserve, such as the one of 1895-96, have been defeated. Those specific to a single project affecting only a small part of the preserve, have been approved.

> The lands of the state, now owned or hereafter acquired, constituting the forest preserve as now fixed by law, shall be forever kept as wild forest lands. They shall not be leased, sold or exchanged, or be taken by any corporation, public or private, nor shall the timber thereon be sold, removed or destroyed.
>
> Article XIV Section 1
> New York State Constitution
>
> THE ASSOCIATION FOR THE PROTECTION OF THE ADIRONDACKS, INC.

The state agency responsible for administration of the Forest Preserve has also changed. The discredited Forest Commission was replaced by the Fisheries, Game and Forest Commission in 1895. In 1900, it became the Forest, Fish and Game Commission. A 1911 law named it the Conservation Commission. In 1927, it was renamed the Conservation Department and, in 1970, the Department of Environmental Conservation.

Even with all these name changes, the administration of the Forest Preserve has continued to be guided by the "forever wild" section of the New York State Constitution. Throughout the years, such administration has been watched over by concerned private organizations and the public to assure this guidance is followed.

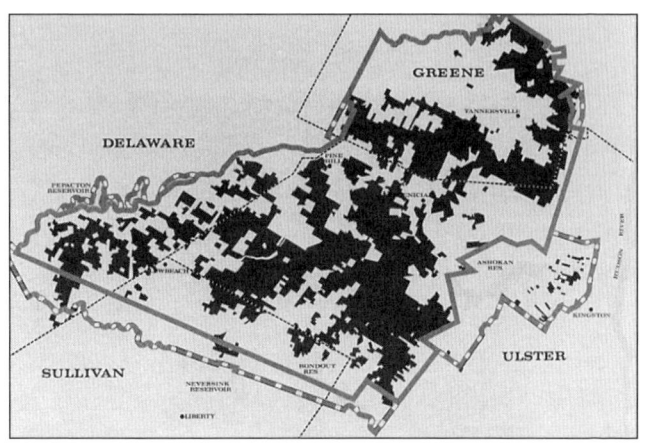

The solid line on this map is the original (1904) "blue line" of the Catskill Park The dashed lines mark the 1957 additions to the park. The dark shaded areas are the lands of the Catskill Forest Preserve as it existed in 1982.

The Catskill Park was created in 1904. Some records say the purpose of the new park was to "embrace a portion of the wild forest lands and within which it was felt the [state's] land acquisition program should be centered." Actually, that isn't correct.

The reason is in the report of another of those long-named legislative committees. The Special Committee of the Senate on the Future Policy of the State in Relation to the Adirondacks and Forest Preservation was studying the small, state-owned parcels of land outside the Adirondack Park. It recommended these parcels be sold. In addition, it said the same program should take place in the Catskills "where no park has yet been laid out." It then recommended "the passage of an act defining the boundaries of the Catskill Park." The 1904 law did just that.

The boundary of the new park was drawn on a map with a blue line similar to that surrounding the Adirondack Park and included 576,120 acres. Thus, the Catskill Park was created not for what was in it, but for what was outside of it.

While legal protection of the Forest Preserve prevented degrading acts by man, it didn't protect against acts of nature.

In 1903, drought and high winds increased the number of forest fires in the Adirondacks. Over 500 were reported. Many were caused by coal-burning, railroad locomotives. Similar conditions continued in succeeding years as did the numbers of forest fires.

In 1909, the first fire observation stations were located on mountain summits. These stations, now called fire towers, were manned during the summer and provided for the early detection of forest fires. No one questioned whether or not these man-made structures were part of "forever wild."

In 1906, white pine blister rust, a tree disease fatal to infected pines, appeared in the Adirondacks and Catskills. The gooseberry plant, the host for the fungi that caused the disease, was targeted for eradication. Teams of men ranged throughout the mountains destroying every gooseberry plant they found. No one raised the question whether or not this wholesale destruction of a plant species was in

Over time, the first rustic observation towers were replaced by steel structures as in these photographs of the original (1909) and current towers on Balsam Lake Mountain in the Catskills.

keeping with "forever wild."

New York's mountain parks have continued to grow.

In 1912, the Adirondack Park was enlarged to over four-million acres to include all of the "Great Forest of Northern New York." In addition, the description of both parks was changed to consist of "all lands located within" the blue line boundaries. This had no immediate effect on the private lands in the two parks, but it would in time.

The Adirondack Park was again expanded in 1931, 1956, and, finally, in 1972 to its present size of 5,927,600 acres.

The Catskill Park has been enlarged only once. In 1957, land easterly to the New York State Thruway near Kingston, southerly into Sullivan County, and westerly to Pepacton Reservoir was added. The Catskill Park now totals 705,500 acres.

The first effect all this had on the private lands in the Adirondack Park was in 1924 when the "signboard law" was enacted. This provided that no advertising sign or billboard could be erected within the park except on property where the advertised business was located. This was to protect "the natural beauty of the Adirondack Park. . . ." In 1969, private lands within the Catskill Park were made subject to the law.

In 1971, the Adirondack Park Agency was created. Under the law, that agency was directed to prepare a plan controlling the development of private lands within the park. It also issued guidelines controlling the uses permitted on those lands and placed restrictions on development along the shorelines of Adirondack lakes and waterways.

The agency and its plan were not well-accepted by the private landowners within the park. Resentment grew and continues to exist throughout the park.

A Catskill Park agency hasn't been created although proposals were made for one in the 1970s.

These signboards confronting the traveler on Route 28 in the Catskills do, indeed, mar "the natural beauty" of the park. Do not also the transmission lines, power pole, and transformer?

Beginning with the $25,000 provided in 1890 to acquire land in the Adirondacks "for the purposes of a state park" a land acquisition program to add to the forest preserves has since been funded almost continuously. The largest dollar amounts have been provided by bond acts approved by the voters in 1924, 1960, 1962, 1972, 1986, and 1996.

One example of a significant land acquisition project is the Moose River Plains in the central Adirondacks. In 1964 a total of over 53,000 acres including the largest winter deer-yarding area in the state was purchased from a single owner (Gould Paper Company). In 1978, over 9,000 acres were acquired from the Adirondack Mountain Reserve (or Ausable Club). This took in all or parts of the summits of eleven peaks over 4,000 feet in elevation and completed state ownership of the upper slopes of all forty-six of these high Adirondack mountains.

The deed closing of this historic state purchase was held on the summit of Noonmark Mountain, one of the peaks included in the title transfer. Among those participating were (left to right): Norman Van Valkenburgh, Department of Environmental Conservation; Anne LaBastille, Adirondack Park Agency; Peter A. Berle, Environmental Conservation Department commissioner; and Arthur Savage & Morgan K. Smith, Ausable Club.

With monies from the 1960-62 bond acts, the state acquired a number of parcels in the North-South Lake area of the northern Catskills. These included the famed, but deteriorated, Catskill Mountain House and 259 acres in 1962. The entire of South Lake was also acquired in 1962. "Rip's Retreat," a ten-acre tourist attraction near the shore of North Lake, was acquired at auction in 1961 by a private organization bidding on behalf of the state. The nearby Laurel House property of over 100 acres was purchased in 1965.

This last acquisition included the famous Kaaterskill Falls, the highest east of the Mississippi River, and the setting of Asher Durand's 1849 painting, *Kindred Spirits*, which depicts Thomas Cole and William Cullen Bryant standing on a ledge looking across to the falls. (This painting recently sold at auction for $35 million.)

As the Forest Preserve and the two parks grew throughout the twentieth century, so too did the articles in New York State's Constitution. The original 1895 "forever wild" language remains but is now an introduction to a longer and more complicated wording. Over 200 amendments have been proposed; however, less than fifty have reached the voters for decision.

Among those approved were a 1927 proposal that allowed the construction of the Whiteface Mountain Memorial Highway that climbs to the summit of that Adirondack peak. A 1948 proposal would have allowed a similar highway up Slide Mountain in the Catskills. Fortunately, this proposal wasn't passed out of the legislature. In 1958, the voters approved the use of 300 acres of Forest Preserve for the routing of the Adirondack Northway.

The Whiteface Memorial Highway, constructed in the mid-1930s, and the Belleayre Mountain Ski Center remain open to the public.

In 1941, approval was given to site the Whiteface Mountain Ski Center on lands of the Adirondack Forest Preserve. In 1947, the use of state lands in the construction of the Gore Mountain Ski Center in the Adirondacks and the Belleayre Mountain Ski Center in the Catskills was approved.

A 1957 constitutional amendment allowed the sale of parcels of Forest Preserve of less than ten acres outside the blue lines of the two parks. In 1973, the ten-acre limitation was increased to 100 acres. Exchanges of small parcels of Forest Preserve for larger parcels of private lands were approved in 1963, 1965, 1983, 1991, 1995, and 2007.

A major land exchange was approved in 1979. This involved 8,500 acres of the Forest Preserve and 10,000 acres owned by International Paper Company at Perkins Clearing in Hamilton County. The two ownerships were scattered in a checkerboard pattern. The exchange consolidated them into two large blocks of land.

The automobile opened up the Forest Preserve to more and more people. The Conservation Commission reported that trails to the fire observation stations "were being utilized and enjoyed by the general public." In 1913, rules were adopted "permitting the construction and use of open camps" known today as lean-tos. The Forest Preserve came to be known as "Nature's Playground."

This and the 1932 Winter Olympic Games scheduled for Lake Placid prompted the so-called "Recreational Amendment." This would have allowed a "single recreational project" on the Forest Preserve. Obviously, this meant the Olympic "bobsleigh run or slide" proposed for state land near Lake Placid. It also would have allowed the construction of "paths, trails, camp-sites and camping facilities" after making "the necessary clearings of timber therefore." The voters defeated the amendment 693,543 to 1,326,599.

Nevertheless, the commission and later departments continued to build and expand recreational facilities on Forest Preserve lands. Public campgrounds now have paved roads, roofed pavilions, sandy beaches where sand never was before, dams, sanitary and water systems, administrative buildings, etc., all constructed within "the necessary clearings of timber therefore."

Didn't the voters in 1932 say all this was unconstitutional?

Mt. Van Hoevenburg "bobsleigh run or slide."

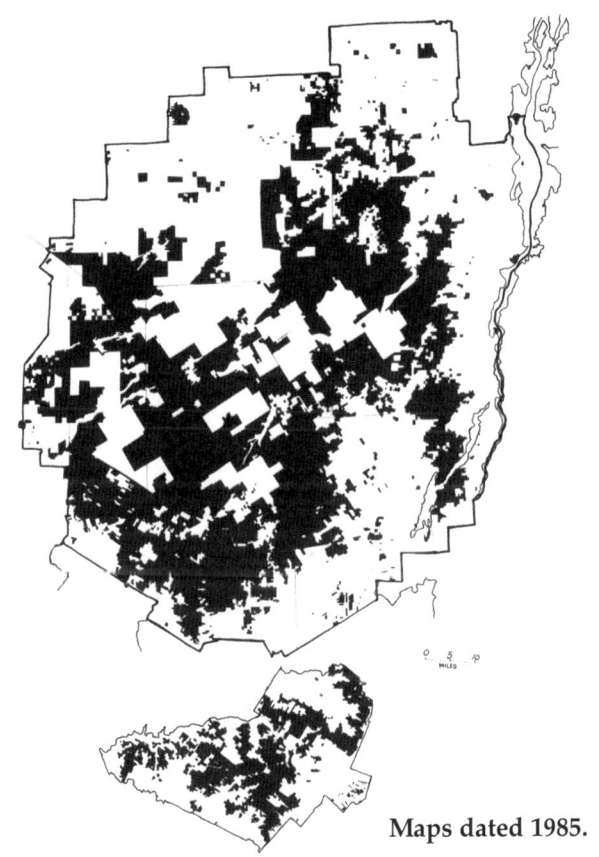

Maps dated 1985.

When the centennial of the Catskill Park was observed in 2004, the Adirondack Park and the two forest preserves had already passed their one-hundredth years. All had grown in size and stature. When created in 1885, the Adirondack Forest Preserve consisted of 681,374 acres. In 2007, it totaled 2,713,734 acres. The Catskill Forest Preserve consisted of 33,894 acres in 1885. By 2007, it had expanded to 290,400 acres. The "blue line" that circled the Adirondack Park in 1892 included 2,800,000 acres. The park has grown to 5,927,600 acres. The Catskill Park, 576,120 acres at its creation in 1904, is now 705,500 acres in size. Who is it that enjoys the benefits of these preserves and parks? Who uses them?

The answer is almost everyone in the eastern part of New York State and those from afar who visit this area.

Some users hike, ride horseback and snowmobiles, cross-country ski, and snowshoe over trails throughout the Forest Preserve. Others picnic, camp, swim, or just relax in the public campgrounds and day-use areas that dot the fringes of the Forest Preserve. Skiers and snowboarders enjoy the slopes of the three state-operated ski centers. Fishermen seek out the ponds and lakes on the preserve while others follow them in season hunting big and small game. Canoers paddle streams small and large while others look for whitewater rapids. Pleasure boaters ply the big lakes. On and on it goes.

What about those who travel the roadways—yes, even up Whiteface Mountain—and marvel at the natural beauty of the high mountain and distant landscapes? Some may never see these forested mountains but are content just knowing they are there and protected for the generations that follow. These, too, share in the benefits of these preserves and parks.

Morning on the Pepacton Reservoir, East Branch of the Delaware River.

However, the major users may not realize who they are. They live in cities and hamlets and drink the water from reservoirs filled by streams beginning on the faraway Forest Preserve. The Catskills alone are the site of five large reservoirs that provide residents of New York City with clean, fresh, and pure water. It is the Forest Preserve that maintains the waters that satisfies their thirst. Every time someone in New York City turns on a water faucet, he or she is enjoying the Forest Preserve. So it is that untold millions benefit in one way or another from New York's Forest Preserves. Each, indeed, owes a debt to those visionaries long ago in the 1800s who conceived this grand experiment of forest and land preservation.

ACKNOWLEDGEMENTS

Without the assistance of the following good people this book would have very few illustrations. Many thanks to Edie Pilcher, Harry Waters, and Patty Prindle of the Adirondack Research Library of the Association for the Protection of the Adirondacks; Aaron Bennett of the Catskill Center for Conservation and Development who, in addition, contributed his photograph of the Ashokan Reservoir and the high mountains beyond which graces the cover; Liz Workman of the Crystal Bridges Museum of American Art, Bentonville, Arkansas; DeAnn Dankowski of The Minneapolis Institute of Arts; John Kettlewell of the Adirondack Mountain Club; Ken Rimany of the Association for the Protection of the Adirondacks, and Judy Adams of the Lowville Free Library, Lowville, New York. Illustrations not otherwise credited are from the author's collection. A special thanks is owed to Kaleigh Sheckler and Troy Demers, a fourth grader and a fifth grader respectively, who read an early draft of the text of the book and surprised me with their understanding of words and phrases I thought might not be part of their vocabularies. If the present text makes sense to young minds it's because of their guidance.

NORM VAN VALKENBURGH
DECEMBER 27, 2007

Another Purple Mountain Press
Educational Book

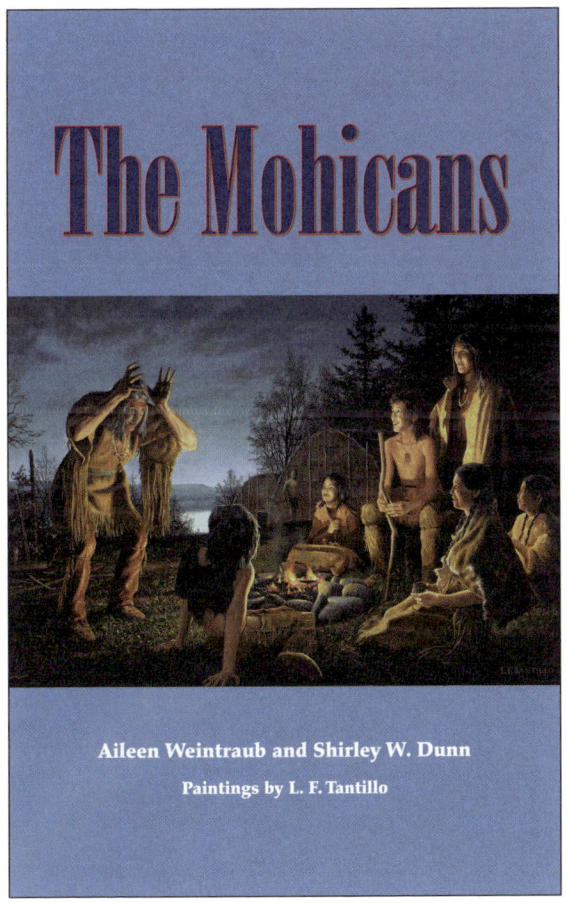

There never was "a last Mohican."

Who are the Mohicans, where did they live, where are they today?

ISBN 978-1-930098-89-3
40 pages, $6.50

Another Purple Mountain Press
Educational Book

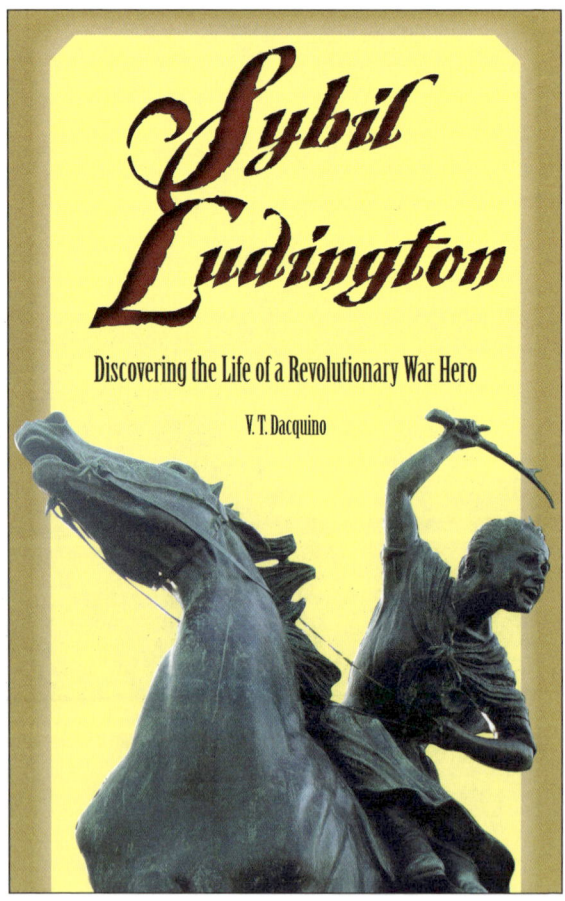

New York's Paul Revere was a sixteen-year-old girl who rode 40 miles on a stormy night to alert her father's troops that the British were coming. Discover her life before and after the famous ride by using documents.

ISBN 978-1-930098-87-9
37 pages, $6.50

Another Purple Mountain Press Educational Book

Four hundred years ago, Henry Hudson and Samuel de Champlain sailed from Europe. This is the story of the two explorers and their quest to find a northern route to the Orient.

ISBN 978-1-930098-90-9
88 pages, $8.50

For a free catalog, write or call or email

PURPLE MOUNTAIN PRESS, LTD.
1060 Main Street, P.O. Box 309
Fleischmanns, NY 12430-0309
800-325-2665, 845-254-4476 (fax), purple@catskill.net

On the Internet: www.catskill.net/ purple